S0-DGG-607

# SERVICES
## —for—
# NATIONAL DAYS

## V. Elaine Strawn &
## Christine L. Nees

Abingdon Press

Services for National Days

Copyright © 1991 by Abingdon Press

Churches and organizations may use the materials in this book without permission from the publisher if 300 or fewer copies are made, provided the following credit line and copyright notice are included:

Reprinted from *Services for National Days* by V. Elaine Strawn and Christine L. Nees. Copyright © 1991 by Abingdon Press. Used by permission.

These materials are not to be reprinted for profit. The book may not be reproduced in whole or in substantial part without permission. Requests should be made in writing and addressed to Abingdon Press, 201 Eighth Ave. South, Nashville, TN 37203.

ISBN 0-687-38095-2

Manufactured in the U. S. A.

# CONTENTS

# INTRODUCTION

Some of the easiest days for pastors to ignore are those days that have national but no sacramental meaning. However, those same Sundays can hold great import for our people, so here we offer orders of worship for the blending of these two points of view. As pastors of local churches, we do well to pay heed to *all* the worship needs of our congregations. This book is intended to serve merely as a collection of possible tools. We hope it will spark your own creativity as you plan for the worship needs of your church people.

In the pages that follow, we have tried to include suggestions for each of the major parts of worship—calls to worship, prayers, litanies, and sermon hints. Each part is centered around the emphasis of the day and includes special ideas for enhancing the worship.

Congregational prayer time has not been developed in the orders of worship because each church has its own format. However, we do suggest that prayers include time for silent prayer and for sharing congregational concerns. In addition to the traditional prayers, we need to allow time for sharing and quiet reflection.

Since many national days do not fall on a regular calendar date, Scripture lessons have been selected in light of their teaching about the theme of the day. Scriptures are provided in the common lectionary for All Saints Day and Thanksgiving, and texts for years A, B, and C have been listed in that order in parentheses: (Year A; Year B; Year C).

We sincerely hope that you find these orders of worship useful as you plan your church year.

# NEW YEAR'S SUNDAY

**GATHERING**

**GREETING**

**CALL TO WORSHIP**

L:  On the very first Sunday of [year], we turn to our God.
P:  **We come to praise, to offer thanks, and to rededicate our lives.**
L:  At the beginning of this year of our Lord, we stop to renew our Covenant.
P:  **The God of all ages has made a commitment to us in the life of Jesus Christ. We offer ourselves, in worship and service, in commitment to our Lord.**

**OLD TESTAMENT**  Isaiah 49:11-18

**HYMN OF PRAISE**

**PRAYERS OF THE PEOPLE with the Lord's Prayer**

**ANTHEM**

**EPISTLE**  Hebrews 8:7-13

**OFFERING with Doxology**

**HYMN OF PREPARATION**

**GOSPEL**  Luke 22:14-23

**MEDITATION**

*A brief sermon may be delivered on beginnings. A new calendar year is beginning, fresh with expectation. Christ also offers us newness and freshness of life, with his new Covenant. This is a good time to reflect on our lives, our commitments, and our resolves. And it is a good time for renewing our vows of covenant with our God.*

**RENEWAL OF COVENANT VOWS**

## INVITATION

The new year, with all its possibilities, awaits us. Again God invites us to renew our covenant, to be part of the chosen people. As people chosen to serve, let us resolve never to cease our prayers of thanksgiving to a generous and merciful God. I invite you to enter into a renewed covenant with our Creator.

## ADORATION in Unison

**O Divine Creator, all that we have and all that we are is yours. We praise you for the beauty of this world; we delight in your meticulous care. Before our eyes, life continues to unfold around us. The generations pass and new generations rise to take their place. Yours is the Voice of wisdom and compassion. You gather us into your loving care and supply us with all that we need. All glory be to you! Amen.**

## CONFESSION

**God of compassion, forgive us. You set before us the model of Christ, but we fail to follow his example. We remain stuck in our own problems, forgetting our hungry, homeless, lonely sisters and brothers. Pride, prejudice, and apathy blind us to the needs of the world around us. Remind us of your vision for the Kingdom. Build us up when our limitations make it seem so hopeless. Enable us to grow beyond the barriers we construct. Make us lovers in a world ripped apart by so much hatred and fear. Continue to believe in us and extend to us your grace. In the name of Christ, our model and our friend, Amen.**

## WORDS OF ASSURANCE

Rejoice! Because of God's infinite grace, you are forgiven. Open yourselves to the Creator's love and go out to surround the world with your loving compassion.

## COVENANT

L: We worship the Creator of all things, One who is full of forgiveness, love, and new possibilities. Our God is worthy of our thanks, and of our commitments.

P: **We are a Covenant people. God has chosen us and continues to choose us; Jesus came to seal the Covenant with love.**

L: As people of the Covenant, we have the unique opportunity to tell the whole world of the love of this great God. We are challenged to embody the good news, to live lives so full of joy, justice, and peace that others also will want to enter into this Covenant with God.

6

**P:** As part of our Covenant agreement, we allow the Spirit of God to have sway in our lives. The Spirit leads us, sometimes where we do not wish to go. Yet God's love is to be with us always; nothing can separate us from God's love. For this we give thanks—with our voices, our lives, and our love. So be it.

Amen.

## SILENT PRAYER

## PRAYER OF THANKSGIVING*

There are no words to express to you our joy and our thanks, O God, for the blessings of the past year and the opportunities of the coming year. When the future overwhelms us, the past haunts us, the present crowds us, make us strong and calm. Let us rest secure in your love and your promise to be with us. In the name of the Spirit of Jesus, our Redeemer and our Brother, Amen.

## HYMN OF DEDICATION

## BENEDICTION

*If Holy Communion is to be celebrated at this service, this prayer may be omitted and the order for communion begun.

# MARTIN LUTHER KING, JR., SUNDAY

## PRELUDE

## INVOCATION in Unison

Great Creator, all of us, of each race and every nation, are your people. Your guidance and caring encompasses the whole world. Your vision extends far beyond our limited imagination and knowledge.

At different times in history, you have sent prophets into our midst to challenge our visions and awaken our humanity. Into our century, you sent Dr. Martin Luther King, Jr., our brother and your servant of justice and peace. We thank you for his example, and we ask that you would kindle in us your passion for righteousness. We pray in the name of Jesus Christ, the Great Liberator of your people. Amen.

## HYMN

## CALL TO CONFESSION from I John 1:7-10

When we live in the light—God's light—we have community with one another. When we say that we do not sin, we deceive ourselves, and God's truth cannot live within us. When we confess our sins, God promises to forgive us and purify us from our wrongdoing. But when we say that we have not sinned, we have none of God's Word in us.

## PRAYER OF CONFESSION

O Great and Compassionate One, look upon the divisions of your people. As Jesus cried for obstinate Jerusalem, so he would cry over the state of our world. Separating us by race and by nation, our fears impair our vision, and we lose our humanity under the weight of greed and self-aggrandizement.

While the messages of Israel's prophets echo in our ears, you continue to call new prophets today. And just as before, they are ignored, mocked, condemned, murdered. Dr. Martin Luther King, Jr., responded to your call of concern for the oppressed people of this country. He sacrificed to bring about equality and justice among us. We honor his courage, yet we have not committed ourselves to his mission.

There is so much to be done! Bind us together in the dream to which he gave voice. Fill us with a passion for justice that will make us tireless workers for your kingdom. In the name of Christ, Amen.

## WORDS OF ASSURANCE from I John 2:9-12

Those who say they are in the light, but hate those around them, are lost in darkness to this moment. Those who are filled with love live in the light, and nothing about them will cause any others to sin. Those who are filled with hatred walk in the darkness and do not know where they are going, for the darkness has made them blind. I write to you, my children, because your sins are forgiven for the sake of Christ.

## ANTHEM

## OLD TESTAMENT   Amos 5:21-24

## PASTORAL PRAYER with the Lord's Prayer

## PRESENTATION OF TITHES AND OFFERINGS with Doxology

## HYMN

## SERMON

*Since this day is devoted to the memory and the ministry of Dr. Martin Luther King, Jr., it would be appropriate to read one of his sermons during this time. Another option would be to concentrate on the impact of Dr. King's message on the world around him. Like Amos and Isaiah, Dr. King preached—and lived—a powerful message of justice. He had the vision to dream dreams of a world united in harmony and equality, where all people could live together. He put his life on the line for God's message.*

*Mention should be made of the other Afro-Americans who gave of their lives and time to improve life in God's great creation. Booker T. Washington, W.E.B. DuBois, Sojourner Truth, Charles Drew, Harriet Tubman, and Rosa Parks are but a few. Our lives would be much less rich without the contributions of these people.*

*All of us are called into action. Jesus read his call to the worshipers gathered in the Temple, and identified himself to them. They could not hear his message, but this did not stop his saving acts. On a different level, God calls each of us into a ministry of love and concern, justice and mercy. The price can be great, but the task is imperative. And the rewards, though often slow in coming, are eternal.*

## LITANY*

**P1:** The church is warm and the pews give us rest, but it is not comfortable to be here.

**P2:** To be present in this place is to dedicate our days to continual vigilance.

**P1:** Our everyday world provides divisions that are common and standard to us. Early in life, we learned these clear separations.

**P2:** But all separations breed inequality, in which God's justice cannot live.

**P1:** In our acquiescence, we lose the chance to receive the gifts of diversity. We miss the enrichment offered by others' differences.

**P2:** From of old, even to the present time, we have heard the prophets' voices. We are indicted by their words.

**All:** May God make us brave. May God make us bold. In the strength of unity, we forge ahead. May the Spirit of God be upon us and fill us with visions of peace.

## HYMN "Lift Every Voice and Sing"**

## BENEDICTION

## POSTLUDE

*In order to give a true sense of the divisions present in our world, divide the congregation by using a characteristic that is often ignored. For example, all the brown- and hazel-eyed people could read P1, while P2 is read by all the blue- and green-eyed people.

**The final hymn was suggested because of its significance as the Black national anthem.

# BOY SCOUT SUNDAY

**GATHERING**

**GREETING**

**PROCESSIONAL HYMN with Christian and U. S. Flags**

**PLEDGE TO THE CHRISTIAN FLAG***

**PLEDGE TO THE U. S. FLAG**

**INVOCATION**

O God of all the generations, be with us as we gather this morning. Just as you have guided our parents and teachers, guide us through the days of our lives. Make us wise in the decisions that face us today, that we may be prepared for the larger decisions we will face in the future. Shelter us in your love, we pray. **Amen.**

**OLD TESTAMENT   Proverbs 4:1-9**

**BOY SCOUTS OF AMERICA PLEDGE**

**MOMENTS OF REFLECTION**

*One boy, or several, may wish to reflect on the ways this organization has affected their lives. Or all the Boy Scouts present may be introduced.*

**PRAYERS OF THE PEOPLE with the Lord's Prayer**

**EPISTLE   I Timothy 4:11-16**

**OFFERING with Doxology**

**HYMN OF PREPARATION**

**GOSPEL   Mark 10:13-16**

**SERMON**

*The minister may choose to reflect on some of the troop's projects, or a troop member may wish to speak. Focus should be placed on the purpose of the Scouting program, and on our need to be prepared for life.*

**PRAYER OF THANKS FOR YOUNG LIVES**

Spirit of wisdom and protection, we are here because you have created us and claimed us as your own. We have witnessed the gifts and talents and growth of these young men this morning. They are yours, and they are also ours—members of our community. Prepare them for the vast future, the possibilities that lie ahead, and go with them every step of the way. Help us to be insightful mentors, who will understand them and direct them with wisdom and love. Amen.

**HYMN OF DEDICATION**

**BENEDICTION**

**RECESSIONAL with both Flags**

*Because of its infrequent use, this pledge may need to be printed:

I pledge allegiance to the Christian flag, and to the [Redeemer/Savior] for whose kingdom it stands: [One family/Brotherhood], uniting all [humanity/mankind] in service and in love.

**Note:** This service should be planned with the troop(s), and the members should take part as readers, ushers, and so on.

# GIRL SCOUT SUNDAY

**GATHERING**

**GREETING**

**PROCESSIONAL HYMN with Christian and U. S. Flags**

**PLEDGE TO THE CHRISTIAN FLAG***

**PLEDGE TO THE U. S. FLAG**

**INVOCATION**

   O God of us all, your creation springs eternal. As each generation reaches full fruition and passes into your arms, a new generation— bright and open and fresh—springs forth, giving us hope. We gather this morning to honor our young women and to thank you for their lives. Open us all to your direction. Make us wise teachers and avid students of your way. Fill us with fresh devotion, guide our steps, and shield us with your love. **Amen.**

**OLD TESTAMENT   Judges 5:6-12a**

## GIRL SCOUTS OF AMERICA PLEDGE

## MOMENTS OF REFLECTION

*Each of the young women may be introduced and/or be invited to comment briefly on aspects of the Scouting program that hold special meaning for her.*

## PRAYERS OF THE PEOPLE with Lord's Prayer

## EPISTLE   Acts 2:14-21

## OFFERING with Doxology

## HYMN OF PREPARATION

## GOSPEL   Matthew 26:6-13

## SERMON

*Many women of the Bible are recognized for their service to others. Deborah offered herself to her people as a judge and a leader. The woman from today's Gospel text gave everything she had to pay homage to Jesus. When Juliet Lowe formed the Girl Guide/Girl Scouting movement, she sought to prepare young women for leadership and service to their communities. Encourage the Girl Scouts' training, and remind the rest of the congregation of its responsibility to aid in the preparation of these young women. The biblical women serve as role models.*

## PRAYER OF THANKS FOR YOUNG LIVES

**O Wonderful Lifegiver, we are awe-stricken when we stop to think of the miraculous workings of your world. You have given us so much. We thank you for the lives of these young women. They fill us with expectancy for the future. Make us worthy and wise guides who not only instruct, but also learn from them. Surround them with your protection and your love, and go with us all as we leave this place.**

**Amen.**

## HYMN OF DEDICATION

## BENEDICTION

## RECESSIONAL with both Flags

*Because of its infrequent use, this pledge may need to be printed:

I pledge allegiance to the Christian flag, and to the [Redeemer/Savior] for whose kingdom it stands: [One family/Brotherhood], uniting all [humanity/mankind] in service and in love.

**Note:** This service should be planned with the troop(s), and troop members should take part as readers, ushers, and so on.

# MOTHER'S DAY / FESTIVAL OF THE CHRISTIAN HOME

## GATHERING AND WELCOME

## CALL TO WORSHIP

L: This is the day set aside to honor women.

**P: We remember Sarah, who laughed at conception, and later gave birth to Isaac; she became the mother of Israel.**

L: We remember Esther, who risked her life to save her people from genocide.

**P: We remember Ruth, who left her home out of devotion to her mother-in-law.**

L: We remember Mary, whose strong sense of love and justice nurtured Jesus.

**P: We remember Anna the prophetess, the woman at the well, and the three women at the tomb, who recognized a vision that the rest of the world missed.**

**All: We honor these women, created in God's image, as well as all the women who have influenced our lives.**

## HYMN

## THE NAMING

*Invite the members of the congregation to recall the women who have nurtured them in their lives and in their faith. This may be followed by silent moments.*

## PRAYER OF THE CONFESSION

**O Lord, forgive us for the times we have ignored the cries of women:**
> **the mothers who watched their children go off to war, and**
> **the wives and friends who were left behind to struggle alone;**
> **the women of faith whose stories we forget;**
> **the women who followed their vision in pursuit of human dignity;**
> **the homemakers who provided nurturing safe space.**

**Make us sensitive to the anguished cries that echo still: the homeless, the poor, the hungry and ill, the lonely, the aged. O God, who loves us like a mother, forgive us. Amen.**

## WORDS OF ASSURANCE

Inasmuch as God has borne us, nursed us, encouraged us to grow, God also will forgive and accept us. God's gift is unconditional love. May we accept this gift as our challenge to go and do likewise. **Amen.**

## OLD TESTAMENT  Genesis 17:15-21; Esther 4:12-17)
### (Sarah and Esther)

## MEDITATION

*Both these women were mothers in an unconventional sense: Sarah, with Abraham, late in life parented God's chosen nation; Esther, although not a biological mother, nurtured her people in a time of threatened extinction. The meditation here might focus on women called by God to be mothers in nontraditional ways.*

## HYMN

### GOSPEL   Luke 1:30-38; Matthew 15:21-28
### (Mary and the Syrophoenician Woman)

## MEDITATION

*Both these women were mothers who faced great odds. Mary's credibility was called into question. Conceiving a child, seemingly out of wedlock, could have meant the end of her betrothal to Joseph, or even death by stoning. The Syrophoenician woman cared so deeply for her sick daughter that she stood alone against Jesus, asking his favor. As he told her later, her faith truly made the child well. Here the meditation might include a listing of the things women give: strength, faith, courage, devotion. Any woman who offers these gifts to others is a role model to us all.*

## PRAYERS OF THE PEOPLE with Prayer Requests, Prayers of Intercession, the Lord's Prayer

## HYMN/ANTHEM

## PRESENTATION OF TITHES AND OFFERINGS with Doxology

## HYMN

## BENEDICTION

Go forth, remembering the women who have nurtured you, and with renewed dedication to the causes of justice and dignity for all.

## POSTLUDE

# MEMORIAL SUNDAY

**GATHERING**

**GREETING**

**CALL TO WORSHIP**

L:   So many memories come to us this weekend;

**P:   So many lives are remembered.**

L:   It is in this place that our hope springs anew.

**P:   This is the gathering space for the people of the resurrection.**

L:   Our memories are joyful because we know that Christ has conquered death.

**P:   Our hearts are thankful for the touch of the people who have gone before us.**

**All: Praise to the Living God!**

**HYMN OF PRAISE**

**OLD TESTAMENT**   Ecclesiastes 3:1-15

**PRAYER OF CONFESSION**

**O Compassionate One, we come to you in this hour seeking solace. We confess that we often forget to love one another until it is too late. Forgive us for our busyness. Teach us to honor our loved ones while they are yet with us. We confess that we often remember this country's wars, but forget the tragic cost to its victims. Remind us to work for peace, that no more blood be shed. Open our hearts to your true loving wisdom, that by truly caring for the living, we may fully honor those who have died. In the name of the One who raised Lazarus from the dead, Amen.**

**WORDS OF ASSURANCE**

When we confess, God listens and responds by restoring our wholeness and removing our guilt. We are forgiven. Thanks be to God!

**ANTHEM**

**EPISTLE**   Revelation 21:1-5

**PRAYERS OF THE PEOPLE with the Lord's Prayer**

**OFFERING with Doxology**

**HYMN OF PREPARATION**

**GOSPEL   John 11:1-3, 17-44**

## SERMON

*This is a weekend which often focuses on death—of the nation's honored warriors and of our personal loved ones. Time is spent decorating gravesites at cemeteries across the country.*

*But this also is a time of much life. Spring has come to full bloom; summer is about to begin, with all its growth and fun. Help the congregation to see the life beyond death, which really is our cause for celebration.*

*Christ showed us that even death could not silence us. Our loved ones who have died have entered a fuller, eternal life. This really should be a time of remembering the lives that touched us but are no longer with us, a time of celebration. We enjoyed the lives those people shared with us. Now they enjoy Life at its ultimate.*

## NAMING LOVED ONES FROM THE PAST

*Invite the congregation to think of people who have particularly blessed them. They may mention the names aloud or silently. You may invite them to the altar to mention the names before God and to offer a quiet prayer of thanks.*

## PRAYER OF THANKSGIVING

Great Creator, we thank you for life's fullness. So many people have blessed us during our lives. Some of them now live with you. We thank you for sharing them with us, and for receiving them into your arms. We thank you that we, too, have endless, abundant life to anticipate. In the name of the Resurrected One, **Amen.**

## HYMN OF DEDICATION

## BENEDICTION

# FATHER'S DAY

**GATHERING**

**GREETING**

**CALL TO WORSHIP**

L:   Our God is great and powerful;
**P:   Yet God is also intimate, drawing us close, like a loving parent.**
L:   God's wisdom is ultimate;
**P:   Yet God listens to each of our concerns.**
L:   The whole earth belongs to God;
**P:   Yet God knows each of us thoroughly, even the number of hairs on our heads.**
**All:  Praise to our Loving God!**

**HYMN OF PRAISE**

**OLD TESTAMENT   I Chronicles 29:10-18**

**PRAYERS OF THE PEOPLE with the Lord's Prayer**

**ANTHEM**

**EPISTLE   Ephesians 6:1-4**

**PRAYER OF CONFESSION**

**O God, you have loved us into being and continue to hold us near. Forgive us when we doubt your love. So often we move away from you, then wonder why you are so far from us. Draw us close to you. Lift us up when we fall, teach us faith when we doubt, help us to love when we feel vengeful. Guide us, O God, for we are your children. Amen.**

**WORDS OF ASSURANCE**

Our Loving God listens when we speak, forgives when we ask, and wipes away our tears when we weep. Rejoice, knowing that you are forgiven.

**OFFERING with Doxology**

**HYMN OF PREPARATION**

**GOSPEL   Luke 15:11-31**

## SERMON

*The story of the prodigal son really tells about a loving father. It is a good example of fatherhood: He allows his son to leave, then forgives the son, rejoicing at his own good fortune when the son receives "new life"—was dead and is alive. The father never says "I told you so!" He even addresses the concerns of his older son. This is a great example for fathers, and for everyone, since God has this kind of forgiveness and love for us.*

## RECOGNITION OF MEN OF THE CHURCH

*(Perhaps have **all** "fathers"—biological, fathers in the faith, teachers, and so on—stand while this is read.)*

This day we honor those fathers who taught us skills and tenderness, played with us and worked for us, loved us and advised us. Today we say thanks to those fathers who worked to provide more than shelter—a home—for their children. Today we honor those fathers who came with their families to church, instead of dropping them off. Today we celebrate those fathers whose love for their children is modeled on God's love for all children. Today we thank God for loving fathers, and for all those men, though not our biological fathers, who have cared for us.

## HYMN OF DEDICATION

## BENEDICTION

# INDEPENDENCE SUNDAY

## GATHERING

## GREETING

## PROCESSIONAL HYMN

*Both the Christian and the U. S. flag are carried in and placed at the front of the sanctuary, crossed, with the Christian flag in front of the U. S. flag.*

## INVOCATION in Unison

**On this summer morning, O Divine Creator, we gather in your holy place to give you thanks and to drink a portion of your wisdom. Bless this nation, its leaders, and all its inhabitants. In this morning worship, draw us closer as a people, and consecrate us afresh as your people. Amen.**

**OLD TESTAMENT** Leviticus 25:8-17

## PRAYER OF CONFESSION

Mighty Ruler, justice is your governing principle. We call ourselves a Christian nation, but we confess our faithlessness. The religious principles on which our nation was founded have turned to self-righteous oppression. Too often, we pray on Sunday and operate without thought of you throughout the week. Wash our eyes, that we may see your visions of justice. Remind us that all people are our sisters and brothers and that when any suffer, we all suffer. Unite us as a nation under your guidance, because all true power resides in you. Amen.

## WORDS OF ASSURANCE

We truly are God's people—chosen and lifted up. We are forgiven and restored. Praise be to God!

**PSALTER READING in Unison: Psalm 119:41-48**

**ANTHEM**

**EPISTLE** James 1:25-27

**PRAYERS OF THE PEOPLE with the Lord's Prayer**

**OFFERING with Doxology**

**HYMN OF PREPARATION**

**GOSPEL** Luke 4:16-21

## SERMON

*We refer to this as a Christian nation, yet we treat our poor, our minorities, and our international neighbors with suspicion. We are a people of the Jubilee, but the profit motive reigns strong. The buildings on the mall in our nation's capital city—the capitol building, the White House, and the three presidential memorials—are arranged in the shape of a cross. We are labeled; we are God's.*

*The message for the morning may focus on the two flags: the Christian flag symbolizes our allegiance and who we are; the U.S. flag symbolizes our mission field, where we are called to act. We are chosen—each of us—to be a minister, to make this nation truly Christian, in the model of the humble Servant Healer who gave his life for justice and love.*

19

## PRAYER FOR DIRECTION

God of Justice and Power, we come to you in our need. We can be so overwhelmed by the grandiosity of life in our country. We feel trivial and powerless. You have written your truths on our hearts. Direct us, so that we may put those truths into action. Fill us with your Spirit of caring, that this may be a nation where all people may be not only free, but may have equal access to food, shelter, health care, and community. Then may we be a beacon to the world, a nation marked by your touch and devoted to your way. Amen.

## HYMN OF DEDICATION

## BENEDICTION

# SUNDAY IN THE PARK

## GATHERING AND WELCOME

## OPENING HYMN

## CALL TO WORSHIP

L:  Come, let us gather to enjoy the beauty of our earth.
P:  **The trees offer shelter, the rains offer relief, the sun gives us energy.**
L:  Tell me of the One who created such beauty and wonder.
P:  **Our God is a lover of beauty, of nourishment, of wholeness.**
L:  We gather to worship the Creator of all that is.
P:  **Praise be to the Creator of Life!**

## OLD TESTAMENT  Psalm 124

## PRAYER OF CONFESSION

O God of plenty, we have squandered the richness of your universe. We have used Earth's resources without regard for tomorrow. We have plundered your nature for our expansion programs, which we label "success." We use Earth's resources to feed the few, while the many starve.

Reach out to us, O God of all Creation. Forgive us for our ignorance and greed. Enlighten us as to your purposes and plans. And teach us to be good stewards of all you have given us for our use. Challenge us to leave your sacred space in better condition than we found it. Amen.

## WORDS OF ASSURANCE

Our God is a God of grace. Just as we are loved with an abundance which provides all the wonder around us, so we are loved without condition. As surely as we gather in God's name, earnestly seeking the better way, so will God be among us, retrieving us from our waste and want, and leading us to wisdom and understanding. **Amen.**

## ANTHEM / FAVORITE HYMN

## EPISTLE   I Corinthians 3:5-17

## PRESENTATION OF TITHES AND OFFERINGS with Doxology

## HYMN

## PRAYERS OF THE PEOPLE with Sharing Concerns, Intercessory Prayer, the Lord's Prayer

## GOSPEL   Matthew 13:1-9

## MEDITATION

*Ask the people to reflect on all the blessings of God's creation. We take so much for granted. How are we like the fig tree? How do we return love to God? Concentrate on the importance of being good stewards on God's earth.*

## INFORMAL TIME OF SHARING / DEDICATION OF OUR GIFTS TO GOD

*Ask the worshipers to think of one gift with which they have been blessed—and then to dedicate that gift to God.*

## HYMN

## BENEDICTION / GRACE OVER THE PICNIC FOOD

# LABOR SUNDAY

**GATHERING**

**GREETING**

**CALL TO WORSHIP**

L:    From all over the world, we come to worship:
**P:    From offices and mines, from hospitals and fields.**
L:    We gather to praise the God of our days,
**P:    Who blesses us with talent and skill, with challenge and meaning.**
L:    Glory be to God, who created all that is,
**P:    And who blesses us with love, with life, and with work.**

**HYMN**

**OLD TESTAMENT**  Deuteronomy 5:12-15

**PRAYER OF CONFESSION**

**You are the God of our lives, O Creator. You fill our days with activity and meaning. You bless us with abilities and call us to service. Forgive us when we fail to answer your call. The noises of the world around us are so loud that we often listen to the voices of greed or apathy, rather than to your call. Be with us in this hour, that we may rededicate our lives to service in your name. Amen.**

**WORDS OF ASSURANCE**

We cry out, and God hears. Our Creator waits for our readiness to act. When we align ourselves with God's plan, our lives blossom and bear fruit. Our God is a God of abundance.

**ANTHEM**

**EPISTLE**  II Thessalonians 3:6-13

**PRAYERS OF THE PEOPLE** with the Lord's Prayer

**OFFERING** with Doxology

**HYMN OF PREPARATION**

**GOSPEL** John 6:25-34

## SERMON

*The focus here may be on the reason we labor. Work is not an end in itself; it is a means of sustaining life so that we may grow. Our work needs to be seen as part of the whole; all work is important, in that it provides needed goods and services. Each person offers something vital to our world. The purpose, however, is not to put labor at the center of our lives. God and our sisters and brothers should be at the center of our lives, while we labor so that all might enjoy God's creation.*

## AFFIRMATION OF FAITH

**We believe in a God who created us and bestowed differing talents upon each of us. God calls us to use these talents for the good of all, building up and supporting one another.**

**We turn to Christ as the example of a fulfilling life. He recognized the needs of people: food, shelter, human love, health and fulfillment. We recognize the same needs and are called to use our talents to those ends.**

**We believe that the Holy Spirit moves us to seek dignity in the workplace: justice, equality, harmony, and understanding. We are called to take our faith commitments into all parts of our lives, including our jobs, that the world may be drawn closer to the Kingdom. Amen.**

## HYMN OF DEDICATION

*Special parts may be added to the hymn to give more attention to Labor Sunday.*

## BENEDICTION

**Note:** Congregants may be invited to dress for the worship service in their work attire, or in clothing that denotes their avocation.

They may be invited to think of a special talent or skill which they particularly wish to offer for God's service. These could be written on a slip of paper (which had been enclosed in the bulletin) and brought to a basket on the altar, following the Affirmation or during the final hymn.

The altar might be adorned with symbols of different vocations: hammers, computers, electric mixers, school books, and so on.

# ALL SAINTS SUNDAY

**GATHERING**

**GREETING**

**PROCESSIONAL HYMN**

**CALL TO WORSHIP**

L:  We gather on the morning of the celebration of All Saints;
**P:  Many have gone before us to pave our way.**
L:  We gather seeking guidance for our lives.
**P:  Many will follow in the path we have trod.**
L:  We are part of the community of God.
**P:  We have a place in the heritage of faith through the ages.**
All: **We gather together to remember our past, to dream of our future, to find nurture for our present.**

**HYMN OF PRAISE**

**FIRST LESSON (Revelation 7:9-17; Revelation 21:1-6a; Daniel 7:1-3, 15-18)**

**PRAYERS OF THE PEOPLE with the Lord's Prayer**

**EPISTLE (I John 3:1-3; Colossians 1:9-14; Ephesians 1:11-23)**

**LIGHTING OF THE CHRIST CANDLE**

*At this time, the leader will light a large white candle placed in the center of the altar or on a table in the chancel, saying something such as, "We light the altar candles each Sunday to remind us of the Living God who abides with us. This morning, we light this white candle to remind us of the Christ who lives with and inside us, forming the central focus of our faith."*

**OFFERING with Doxology**

**HYMN OF PREPARATION**

**GOSPEL (Matthew 5:1-12; John 11:32-44; Luke 6:20-36)**

## SERMON

*The sermon this morning may bring together the two holidays—secular Halloween and sacred All Saints Day. Ancient lore held that Halloween was the time when the spirit world and the world of the living came closest together.*

*This lore could be used in our Christian service. One of the signposts of our faith is resurrection—the crucified Savior raised to life. We are a resurrection people. Our loved ones are not dead; they have been raised with Christ, who sent the Holy Spirit to dwell among us. The heavenly world, where we will meet those who have gone before, is never far from us. So the two holidays are not so different, after all.*

## NAMING OUR SAINTS

*Congregants may receive small candles (tea lights work very well) as they enter the sanctuary, or they may be passed out in the pews. All who wish may come forward at this time to light their candles at the Christ candle and name their "saints"—the departed who have left a lasting impression upon these people's lives. The candles may be left on the altar or on a table in the chancel area.*

## AFFIRMATION OF FAITH

Our lives were given to us by God the Creator. We are endowed with special gifts and graces for use in God's plan for the universe.

The possibilities of life were expanded by the life of Christ, God-with-us. He showed us life beyond the limits of sickness, poverty, even death.

Our lives are lived in community in the Spirit of God, the spark of the divine in each of us, and we are bound together in the Church—past, present, future. Saints have gone before us, just as we go before the next generation. The God of the Ages will raise us all to eternal life. Amen.

## HYMN OF DEDICATION

## BENEDICTION

**Note:** The Scripture lessons used in this service are taken from the lectionary, and are listed in order of the year: (A; B; C).

# ELECTION SUNDAY

**GATHERING**

**GREETING**

**INVOCATION in Unison**

O God of the Nations, look upon us as we gather this morning. Revive us from weariness, clear our confusion, ignite our passion for justice, and lead us forward as a people, devoted to you and to your nation. Amen.

**HYMN OF PRAISE**

**OLD TESTAMENT   I Samuel 10:17-25**

**PRAYER OF CONFESSION**

O Great Source of Wisdom, we come to you today, a people confused and troubled. Our country is so big that we no longer know our elected officials. So much corruption fills the news that we become too disillusioned to care. We confess that we grow complacent in our choices and in our duties; the system is too big for the left hand to know what the right is doing. We feel confused and apathetic. Forgive our indifference and help our hopelessness. Remind us whose world this is. Bless us with wisdom, that our voting and our actions may bring us closer to our ideal of a country devoted to you. Amen.

**WORDS OF ASSURANCE**

Jesus reminds us to give to Caesar what is his and no more. Reclaim your rights and your power to help this country's future. You stand forgiven and restored as a people of God, citizens of the Kingdom.

**ANTHEM**

**EPISTLE   Ephesians 1:15-23**

**PRAYERS OF THE PEOPLE with the Lord's Prayer**

**OFFERING with Doxology**

**HYMN OF PREPARATION**

**GOSPEL   Matthew 22:15-22**

## SERMON

*Separation of Church and State is a primary principle of this country's governance. This does not mean, however, that we need not turn to God for wisdom at all times, especially in times of crucial decision-making. The priests of Israel were always consulted when their country needed a ruler. Our God is not aloof from us, but is concerned about our day-to-day lives. God's wisdom is so much greater than ours. Why do we not use it?.*

## PRAYER OF INTERCESSION

God of Time and Place, your caring for this world knows no limit. We turn to you in this hour, asking you to bless our nation. Make it a place where people are respected and treated fairly, regardless of race, belief, sex, or preference. Build in us a burning desire to provide for the needs of people, so that all may live abundantly. Make us good neighbors in the international community; help us to seek the good of all, rather than the benefit of the few. We pray for our nation's leaders. Give them wisdom, patience, insight, compassion. Guide and protect them. Let them know both your power and your love. **Amen.**

## HYMN OF DEDICATION

## BENEDICTION

# VETERANS SUNDAY

**GATHERING**

**GREETING**

**INVOCATION in Unison**

On this day we come before you, God of All Peoples. We remember those who have given their lives in the name of freedom, and those who have struggled for peace. We honor those who have sacrificed much in the cause of equality, and those who continue to lead us toward harmony. Bless this hour. Make this time of worship a time of examination, reflection, and rejuvenation. Amen.

**HYMN OF PRAISE**

**OLD TESTAMENT   Isaiah 11:1-9**

**PRAYER OF CONFESSION**

O Merciful One, we confess to our failures. We have allowed our prejudices to blind us to the commonality of all people. We have embraced our fears and insecurities, rather than surrendering them to your ideals of love and harmony. Ours is a world of such opposing information that it is often difficult to find the truth. Forgive us when we allow self-pride to stand in the way of human concern. Bind us together, one people throughout your creation. In the name of Christ, the Bridge-builder, Amen.

**WORDS OF ASSURANCE**

Nothing we do will separate us from God's infinite love. Knowing that you have been forgiven, you will be able to go forth to embrace the world.

**EPISTLE   Ephesians 6:10-20**

**PRAYERS OF THE PEOPLE with the Lord's Prayer**

**OFFERING with Doxology**

**HYMN OF PREPARATION**

**GOSPEL   Luke 22:14-23**

## SERMON

*Our world is so confusing. There is more information than we can absorb, and much of it is contradictory. It is hard to know which is the side of righteous action. On this day we honor people who have offered their lives in action for what they considered to be just causes. As we honor them, we also must commit ourselves to action. Our world is in need of faithful prayer partners, knowledgeable voters and activists, volunteers, educators, and good neighbors. Without our actions for world harmony and justice, veterans of all types of crusades will have died in vain. Our mission is not complete until the needs of the whole world's population are met and all people are self-determining. We must listen closely for the Spirit's wisdom and guidance in ways of peace, so that in the future of our world, it will not be necessary that people die for justice and peace.*

## ACT OF COMMITMENT

L: Let us join in committing ourselves to action in the causes of justice, peace, equality, and human concern:

**All: We commit ourselves to act for God's kingdom of peace and justice. In areas where inequality causes hunger and suffering, we commit ourselves to work for change. In areas where people are not free, we pledge our action to obtain that freedom. In areas where people are discriminated against, we vow to work for their equality. We pledge to undergird the world with our prayers. We promise to keep our hearts open to the peoples of the world, so that their need does not escape us. We pledge involvement; our actions and influence will be used to restore God's creation to justice, harmony, and shalom. Amen.**

## PRAYER in Unison

**Gracious God, we thank you this day for all your servants who loved freedom so much that they jeopardized their lives for others. We thank you for that within us which yearns for peace, for justice, and for freedom—for ourselves and for others. We pray for these gifts for everyone in the world. May war become unnecessary and oppression obsolete. Keep strong within us the desire to work for your peace and your shalom, today and everyday. In Jesus' name, Amen.**

## HYMN OF DEDICATION

## BENEDICTION

**Note:** Veterans might participate as liturgists, ushers, greeters, and so on, in this service. They may wish to wear their service uniforms. Some may be invited to share either a joy or a concern about world peace and freedom. Several service groups are often ignored during this time; do not forget the women veterans, the health-care workers, the conscientious objectors who served their country, and the volunteers. People who have been involved in peace efforts may also want to share in the service.

# THANKSGIVING SUNDAY

**GATHERING**

**GREETING**

**CALL TO WORSHIP**

L:  We gather to rejoice in the bounty of our God.
**P:  Yahweh brought us out of slavery and into the Promised Land.
Praise be to Yahweh!**
L:  We gather to give thanks for all the blessings of our lives.
**P:  Our God cares for us beyond measure, providing all that we
need. Thanks be to our God!**
L:  We gather to listen for the call of the Spirit, directing us in our
mission of caring for the world.
**P:  The Spirit calls. Let us not be slow to answer.**

**HYMN OF PRAISE**

**OLD TESTAMENT  (Deuteronomy 8:7-18; Joel 2:21-27;
Deuteronomy 26:1-11)**

**PSALM OF PRAISE  Read Responsively (Psalm 65; Psalm 126;
Psalm 100)**

**SPECIAL BLESSING OVER SHARED GIFTS***

O Giver of Abundant Life, we thank you for your many good gifts
to us—life, family, friends, sorrows, joys. All that we have and all that
we are is yours. Yet we know that you are happy when we offer to you
some of those gifts.

Bless these things we place before you now. May this giving be only
the beginning of our ways to share with others the Good News of your
love. Help us to give freely out of our abundance, rather than from
our leftovers. And make us generous, we pray in the name of your
generous gift, Jesus Christ. Amen.

**ANTHEM**

**PRAYERS OF THE PEOPLE with the Lord's Prayer**

**EPISTLE  (II Corinthians 9:6-15; I Timothy 2:1-7;
Philippians 4:4-9)**

**OFFERING with Doxology**

## HYMN OF PREPARATION

## GOSPEL   (Luke 7:11-19; Matthew 6:25-33; John 6:25-35
[or Luke 12:22-31])

## SERMON

*In our work-a-day world, we worry about our bills, our credit cards, our overtime, and our benefits. All these are necessities of our modern world, but when we lose perspective, they assume giant proportions and threaten to smother us under their weight.*

*At this time of year, Christ invites us to study the lilies of the field. We are invited to take stock of the many blessings we take for granted every day. Often when the world seems most dreary, some unexpected hope shines out in front of us.*

## LITANY OF THANKSGIVING

L:   With food and home and clothing,
**P:   Lord, you nourish us and make us whole.**
L:   With family and friends and all who support us,
**P:   Lord, you nourish us and make us whole.**
L:   With meaningful vocations and avocations, with action and purpose in our lives,
**P:   Lord, you nourish us and make us whole.**
L:   With community and nation, with freedom of speech and choice,
**P:   Lord, you nourish us and make us whole.**
**All:   O Lord of all the Universe, challenge us to use all these, your gifts, to extend your bounty and care to all who are in need. Open our eyes, our ears, and our minds to your leading and direction. Amen.**

## HYMN OF DEDICATION

## BENEDICTION

*The congregation might be asked to bring canned goods and paper products, or items of warm clothing. These may be used to decorate the altar and blessed at this time, or they could be brought forward at this point.

**Note:** The Scripture lessons used in this service are taken from the lectionary and are listed in order for the years: (A; B; C). An additional suggestion is made for the Gospel lesson.